LEARN TO DRAW...
CUTE THINGS!

Illustrated by Kerren Barbas Steckler

Designed by Heather Zschock

PETER PAUPER PRESS, INC.
White Plains, New York

For Emily and Audrey

PETER PAUPER PRESS

In 1928, at the age of twenty-two, Peter Beilenson began printing books on a small press in the basement of his parents' home in Larchmont, New York. Peter—and later, his wife, Edna—sought to create fine books that sold at "prices even a pauper could afford."

Today, still family owned and operated, Peter Pauper Press continues to honor our founders' legacy of quality, value, and fun for big kids and small kids alike.

Illustrations copyright © 2020 Kerren Barbas Steckler
Designed by Heather Zschock

Copyright © 2020
Peter Pauper Press, Inc.
Manufactured for Peter Pauper Press, Inc.
202 Mamaroneck Avenue
White Plains, NY 10601 USA
All rights reserved
ISBN 978-1-4413-3439-8
Printed in China

Published in the United Kingdom and Europe by
Peter Pauper Press, Inc. c/o White Pebble International
Unit 2, Plot 11 Terminus Road
Chichester, West Sussex PO19 8TX, UK

7 6 5 4

Hey, young artists!

Are you ready to
learn how to draw
53 super-cute things?
It's easy and fun!
Just follow these steps:

. . . .

First, pick something adorable you want to draw.

Next, trace over the picture with a pencil. This will give you a feel for how to draw the lines.

Then, following the numbers, start drawing each new step (shown in red) of the picture in the empty space in each scene, or on a piece of paper.

Lastly, if you're an awesome artist (and of course you are!), try drawing a whole scene with one or more cute things. And remember, don't worry if your drawings look different from the ones in this book—no two adorable works of art are exactly alike!

You're on your way to creating your own special masterpieces!

GET READY! GET SET! DRAW!

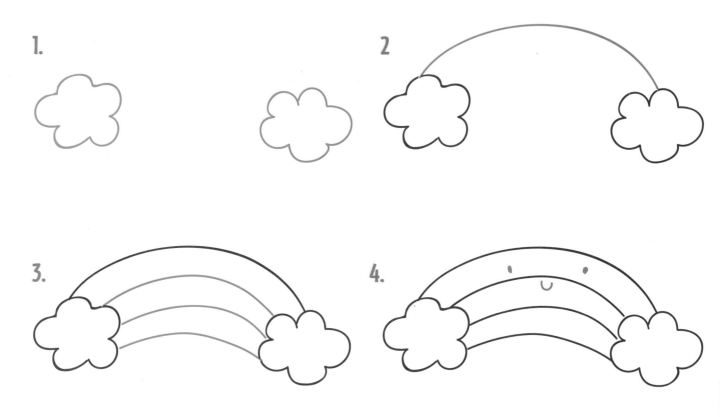

Trace over us
for practice!

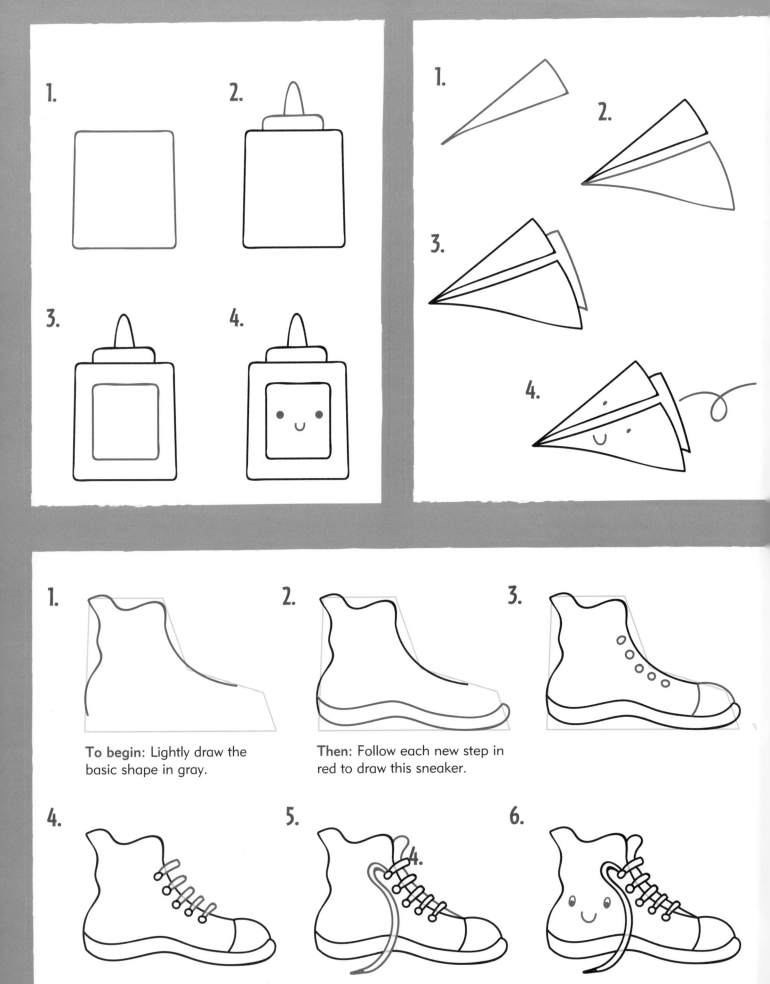

1.

2.

3.

4.

1.

2.

3.

4.

1.

To begin: Lightly draw the basic shape in gray.

2.

Then: Follow each new step in red to draw this sneaker.

3.

4.

5.

4.

6.

Trace over us for practice!

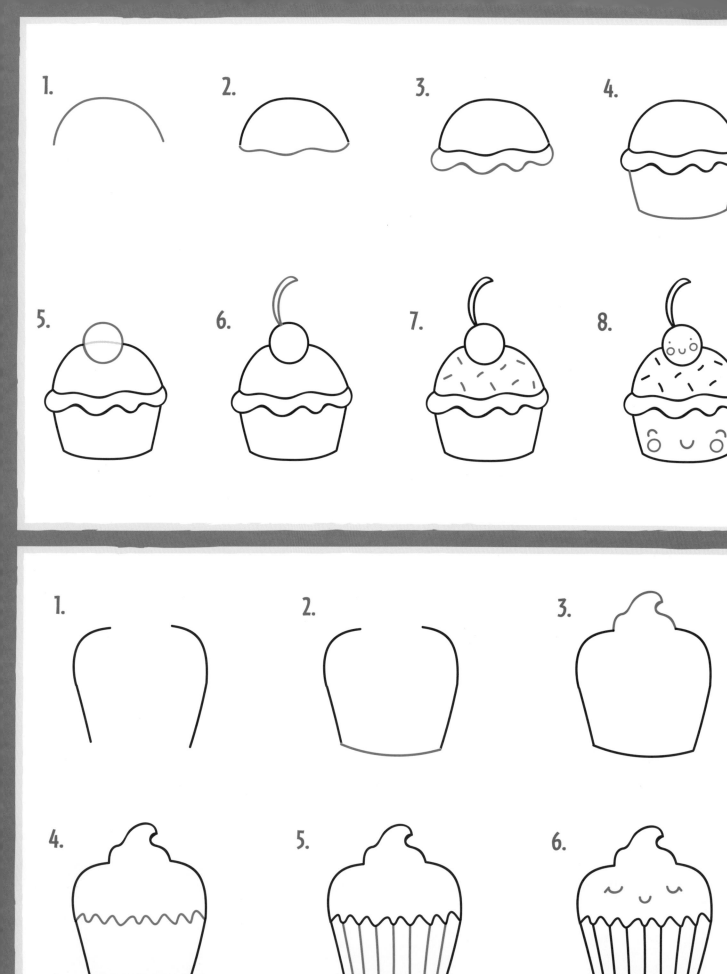

Trace over us for practice!

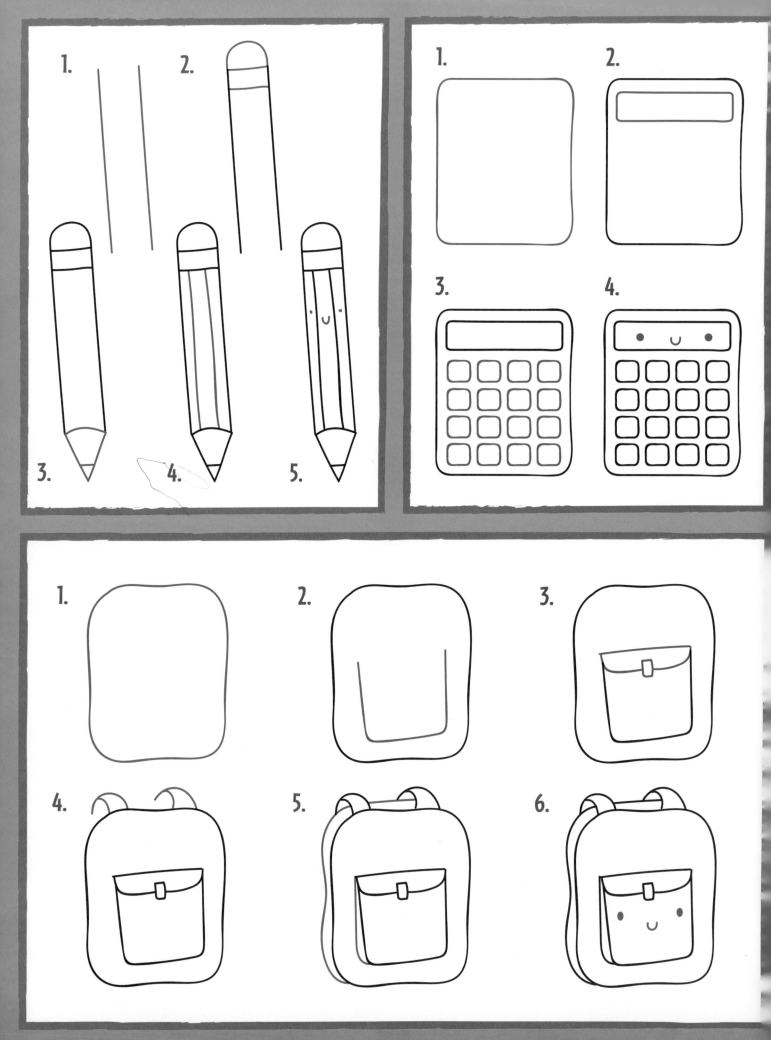

Trace over us for practice!

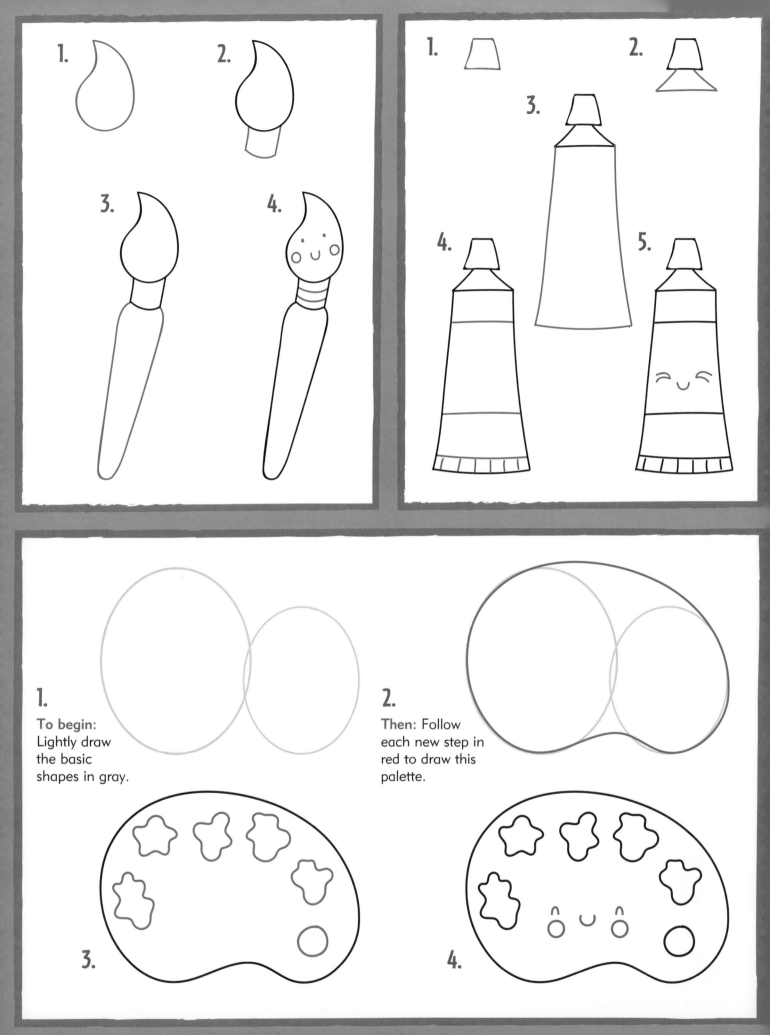

1.

2.

3.

4.

1.

2.

3.

4.

5.

1.

To begin:
Lightly draw
the basic
shapes in gray.

2.

Then: Follow
each new step in
red to draw this
palette.

3.

4.

Trace over us for practice!

1.  2.

3.  4.

5.  6.

1.

2.

3.

4.

1. **To begin:** Lightly draw the basic shapes in gray.

2. **Then:** Follow each new step in red to draw this pear.

3.  4.

1.  2.

3.  4.

Trace over us
for practice!

1. To begin: Lightly draw the basic shapes in gray.

2. Then: Follow each new step in red to draw this star.

3.

4.

1.

2.

3.

1.
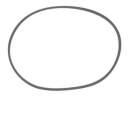

2.

3.

4.
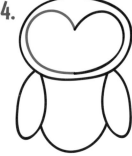

5.

6.

7.

8.

1.

2.

3.

4.

5.

6.

1.

2.

3.

4.

5.

6.

7.

8.

Trace over us for practice!

Trace over us for practice!

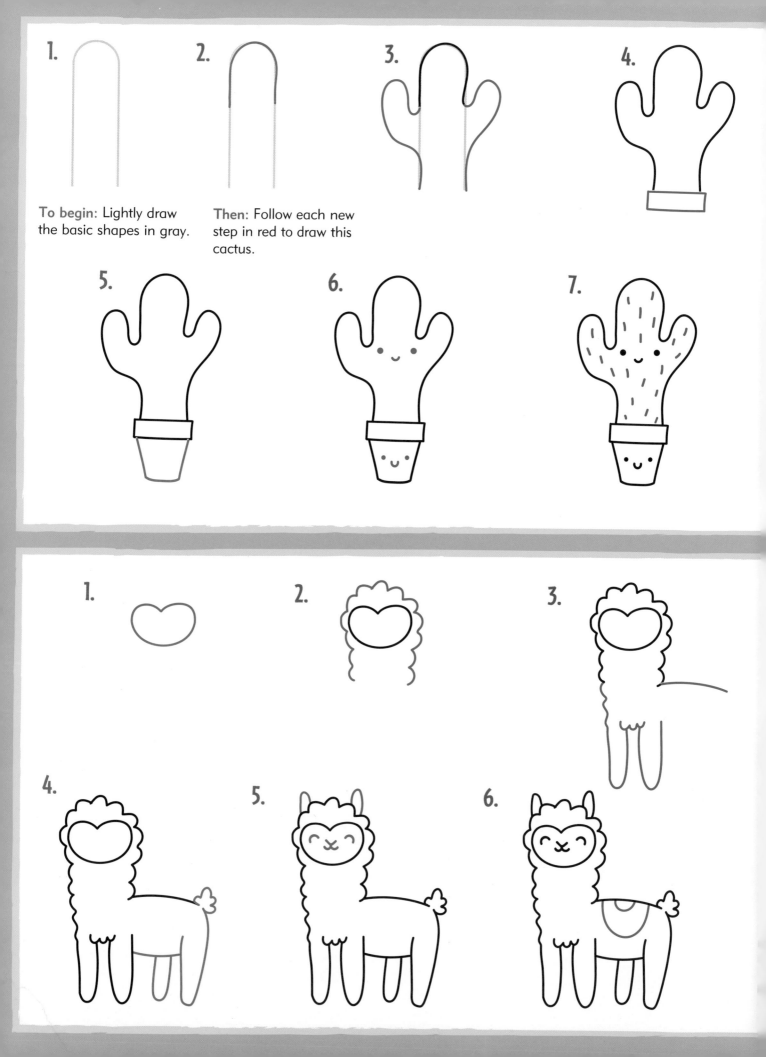

1.

2.

To begin: Lightly draw
the basic shapes in gray.

Then: Follow each new
step in red to draw this
cactus.

3.

4.

5.

6.

7.

1.

2.

3.

4.

5.

6.

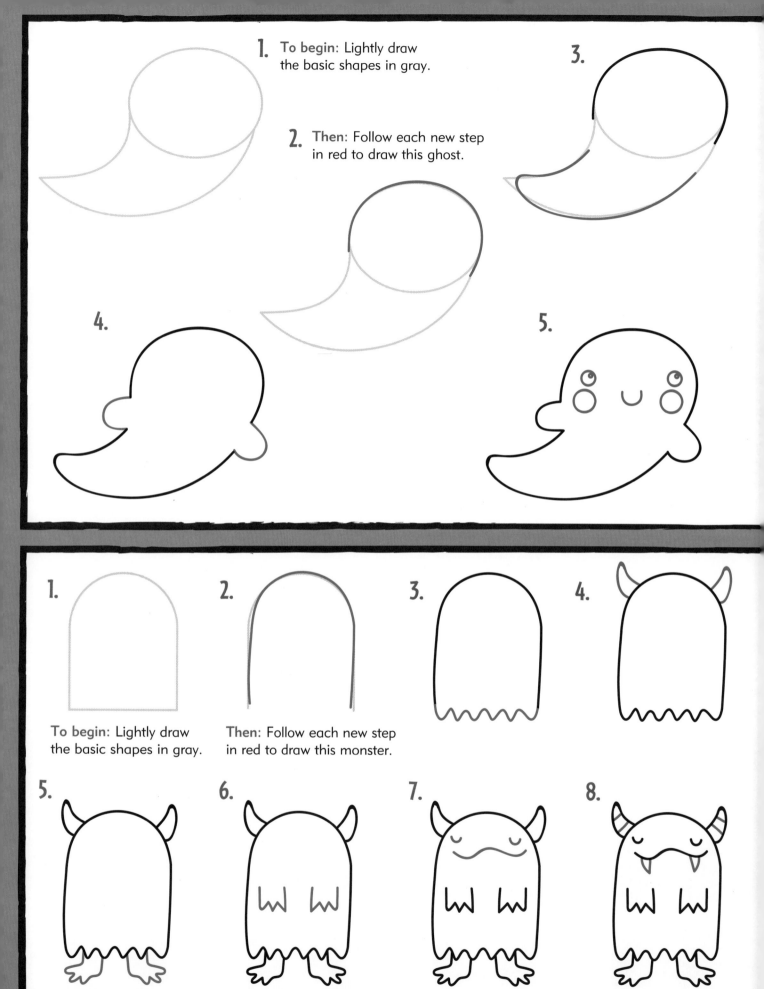

1. To begin: Lightly draw the basic shapes in gray.

2. Then: Follow each new step in red to draw this ghost.

3.

4.

5.

1. To begin: Lightly draw the basic shapes in gray.

2. Then: Follow each new step in red to draw this monster.

3.

4.

5.

6.

7.

8.

Trace over us for practice!

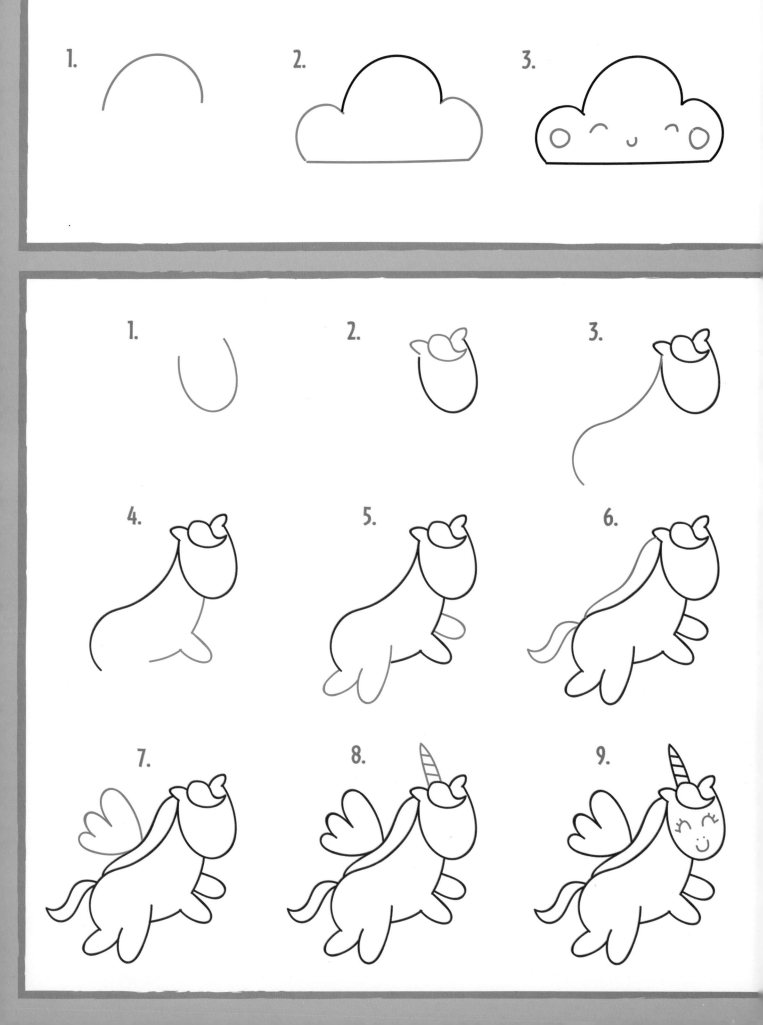

Trace over us for practice!

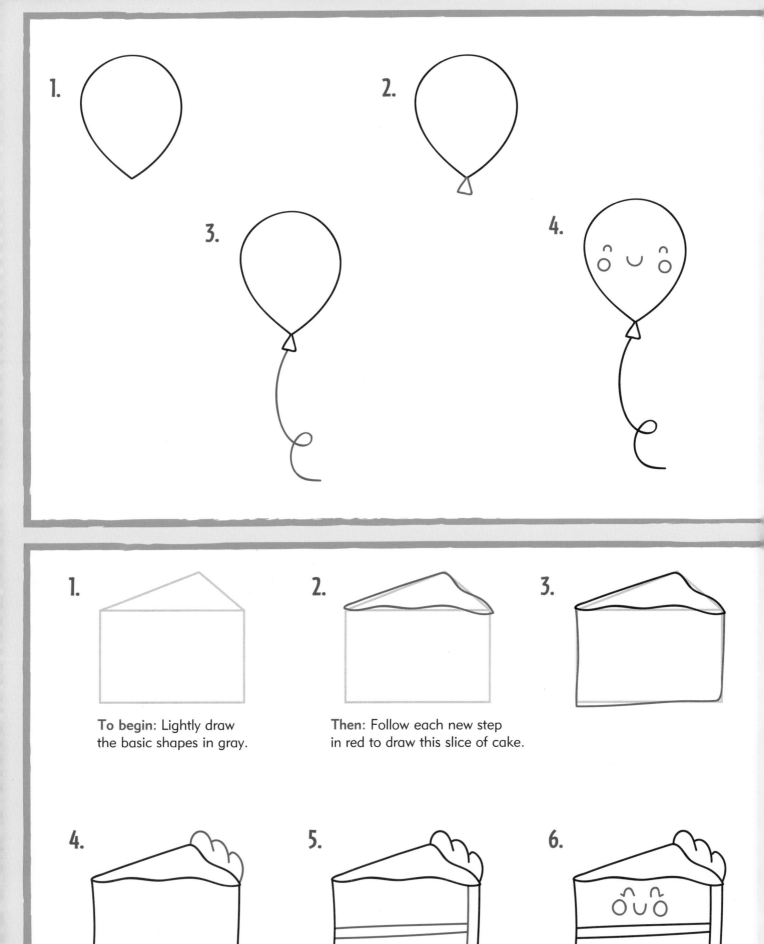

1.

2.

3.

4.

1.

To begin: Lightly draw the basic shapes in gray.

2.

Then: Follow each new step in red to draw this slice of cake.

3.

4.

5.

6.

1. **To begin:** Lightly draw the basic shapes in gray.

2. **Then:** Follow each new step in red to draw this bunny.

3.

4.

5.

6.

1.

2.

3.

To begin: Lightly draw the basic shapes in gray.

Then: Follow each new step in red to draw this fox.

4.

5.

6.

7.

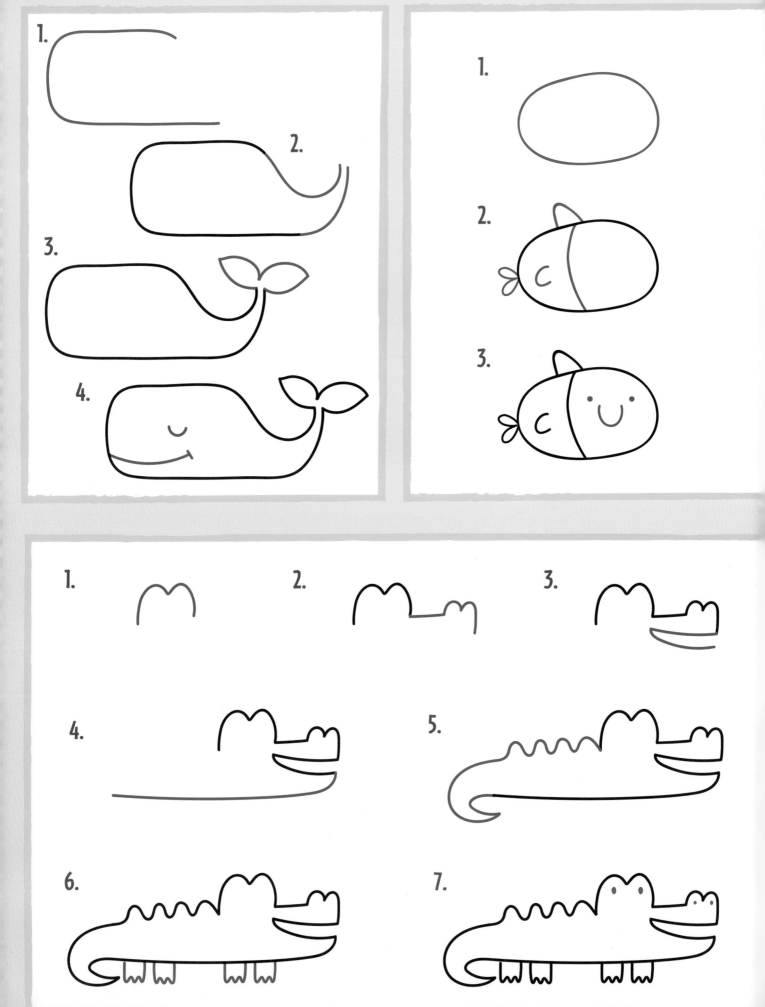

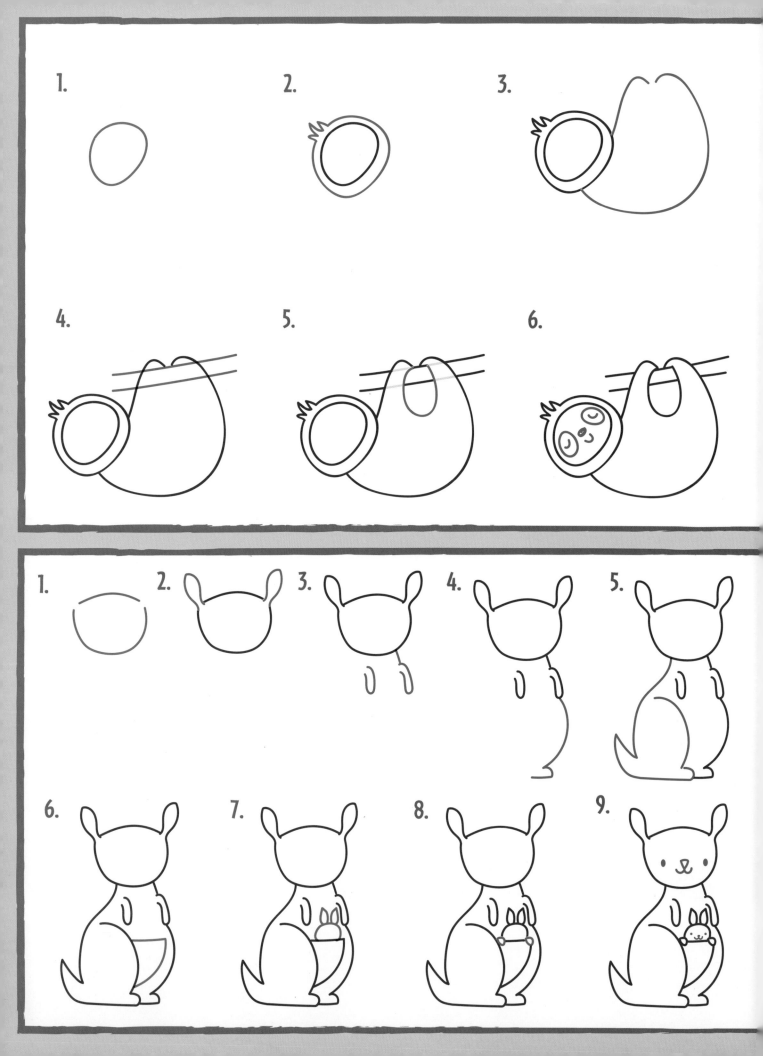

1.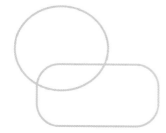

2.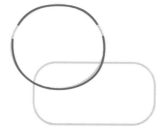

3.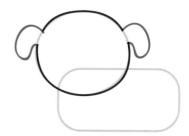

To begin: Lightly draw
the basic shapes in gray.

Then: Follow each new step
in red to draw this dog.

4.

5.

6.

1.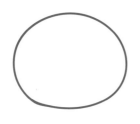

2.

3.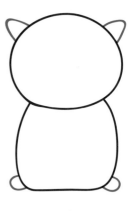

4.

5.

6.

1.

2.

3.

4.

5.

6.

7.

1.

2.

3.

4.

5.

6.

Trace over us for practice!

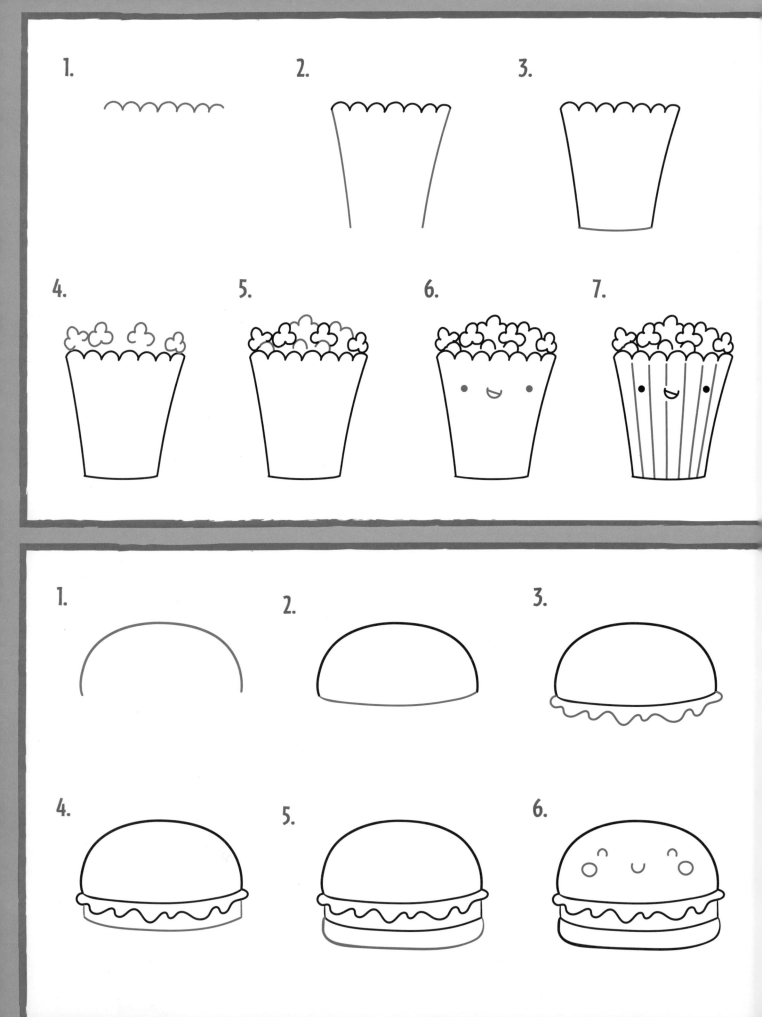

1.

2.

3.

4.

5.

6.

7.

1.

2.

3.

4.

5.

6.

Trace over us for practice!

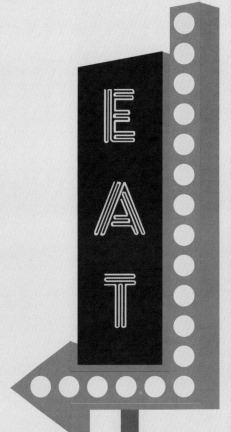

We've reached the end,
and now we're done.

Drawing cute things
is so much fun!